RUINS AND VISIONS

POEMS 1934-1942

BOOKS BY STEPHEN SPENDER

Ruins and Visions

POEMS 1 9 3 4 – 1 9 4 2

by Stephen Spender

RANDOM HOUSE · NEW YORK

FIRST PRINTING

Manufactured in the United States of America
American Book–Stratford Press, Inc., New York, N. Y.

THE STILL CENTRE

[6]

RUINS AND VISIONS

The Still Centre

TO

INEZ

The Still Centre contains nearly all the shorter poems I have written since the publication of the second edition of my book of *Poems*, in September, 1934, and prior to the publication of *Ruins and Visions*.

I have eliminated a few poems which I did not think worth reprinting. Besides which, I have entirely rewritten some of those with which I was not satisfied; notably those appearing here under the titles *Exiles from Their Land, History Their Domicile; An Elementary School Class Room in a Slum;* and *The Uncreating Chaos.*

The poems are printed in the order of development, rather than in the exact order in which they were written. To make the stages of development clearer, I have divided the book into four sections.

The earliest poems—those in Part One—are for the most part written round subjects, and worked out with considerable elaboration. The poems in the Second and Third Parts, written for the most part during a time when I was preoccupied with various kinds of political activity, are more occasional, and written directly and fairly quickly from the experiences which suggested them.

I have printed the Third Part separately, instead of including it in the Second Part, because all these poems are concerned with the Spanish War. As I have decidedly supported one side—the Republican—in that conflict, perhaps I should explain why I do not strike a more heroic note. My reason is that a poet can write only about what is true to his own experience, not about what he would like to be true to his experience.

Poetry does not state truth, it states the conditions within which something felt is true. Even while he is writing about the little portion of reality which is part of his experience, the poet may be conscious of a different reality outside. His problem is to relate the small truth to the sense of a wider, perhaps theoretically known, truth outside his experience. Poems exist within their own limits, they do not exclude the possibility of other things, which might also be subjects of poetry, being different. They remain true to experience and they establish the proportions of that experience. One day a poet will write truthfully about the heroism as well as the fears and anxiety of today; but such a poetry will be very different from the utilitarian heroics of the moment.

I think that there is a certain pressure of external events on poets today, making them tend to write about what is outside their own limited experience. The violence of the times we are living in, the necessity of sweeping and general and immediate action, tend to dwarf the experience of the individual, and to make his immediate environment and occupations perhaps something that he is even ashamed of. For this reason, in my most recent poems, I have deliberately turned back to a kind of writing which is more personal, and I have included within my subjects weakness and fantasy and illusion.

Versions of many of these poems have appeared before, in The Listener, Spectator, New Statesman and Nation, New Verse, New Writing, The London Mercury, Poetry, The Year's Poetry, and The Faber Book of Modern Verse. I make the usual acknowledgements to the editors concerned; and to Mr. John Lehmann, my fellow editor of Poems of Spain.

[12]

PART ONE

POLAR EXPLORATION

Our single purpose was to walk through snow
With faces swung to their prodigious North
Like compass iron. As clerks in whited banks
With bird-claw pens column virgin paper,
To snow we added foot-prints.
Extensive whiteness drowned
All sense of space. We tramped through
Static, glaring days, Time's suspended blank.
That was in Spring and Autumn. Summer struck
Water over rocks, and half the world
Became a ship with a deep keel, the booming floes
And icebergs with their little birds:
Twittering Snow Bunting, Greenland Wheatear,
Red-throated Divers; imagine butterflies
Sulphurous cloudy yellow; glory of bees
That suck from saxifrage; crowberry,
Bilberry, cranberry, Pyrola Uniflora.
There followed Winter in a frozen hut
Warm enough at the kernel, but dare to sleep
With head against the wall—ice gummed my hair!
Hate Culver's loud breathing, despise Freeman's
Fidget for washing: love only the dogs
That whine for scraps, and scratch. Notice
How they run better (on short journeys) with a bitch.
In that, different from us.
Return, return, you warn. We do. There is

A network of railways, money, words, words, words.
Meals, papers, exchanges, debates,
Cinema, wireless: the worst, is Marriage.
We cannot sleep. At night we watch
A speaking clearness through cloudy paranoia.
These questions are white rifts:—Was
Ice our anger transformed? The raw, the motionless
Skies, were these the Spirit's hunger?
The continual and hypnotized march through snow,
The dropping nights of precious extinction, were these
Only the wide inventions of the will,
The frozen will's evasion? If this exists
In us as madness here, as coldness
In these summer, civilized sheets: Is the North,
Over there, a tangible, real madness,
A glittering simpleton, one without towns,
Only with bears and fish, a staring eye,
A new and singular sex?

EASTER MONDAY

The corroded charred
Stems of iron town trees shoot pure jets
Of burning leaf. But the dust already
Quells their nervous flame: blowing from
The whitening spokes
Of wheels that flash away
And roar for Easter. The city is
A desert. Corinthian columns lie
Like chronicles of Kings felled on their sides
And the Acanthus leaf shoots other crowns
Of grass and moss. Sands and wires and glass
Glitter in empty, endless suns. . . . And
In the green meadows, girls in their first
Summer dresses, play. The hurdy-gurdy noise
Trumpets the valley, while egg-freckled arms
Weave their game. Children gather
Pap-smelling cowslips. Papers
Weightless as clouds, browse on the hills.
The bourgeois in tweeds
Holds in his golden spectacles'
Twin lenses, the velvet and far
Mountains. But look, rough hands
From trams, 'buses, bicycles, and of tramps,
Like one hand red with labour, grasp
The furred and future bloom
Of their falling, falling world.

EXPERIENCE

What the eye delights in, no longer dictates
My greed to enjoy: boys, grass, the fenced-off deer.
It leaves those figures that distantly play
On the horizon's rim: they sign their peace, in games.
What is put away, stays removed: music which taps
The soft drums of the ear, I do not sleep with
Though whispering through my blood. Why should faces
    I pass,
Lights under evening trees, bewilder the breath
Which is a noteless, perpetual engine? Make mind re-
    consider
Projects?

There was a wood,
Habitation of foxes and fleshy burrows,
Where I learnt to uncast my childhood, and not alone,
I learnt, not alone. There were four hands, four eyes,
A third mouth of the dark to kiss. Two people
And a third not either: and both double, yet different.
I entered with myself. I left with a woman.

Good-bye now, good-bye: to the early and sad hills
Dazed with their houses, like a faint migraine.
Orchards bear memory in cloudy branches.
The entire world roared in a child's brain.
It suffers accidents. Now I am yours.
My questions only had their answer
When they were fully put.
    'There are two questioners, two answerers,
They must meet in a wood.'
The question, the answer
Were never yours or mine, but always, ours.

EXILES FROM THEIR LAND, HISTORY
THEIR DOMICILE

History has tongues
Has angels has guns—has saved has praised—
Today proclaims
Achievements of her exiles long returned
Now no more rootless, for whom her printed page
Glazes their bruised waste years in one
Balancing present sky.

See how her dead, like standards
Unfurled upon their shore, are cupped by waves:
The laurelled exiles, kneeling to kiss these sands.

Number there freedom's friends. One who
Within the element of endless summer,
Like leaf in amber, petrified by light,
Studied the root of action. One in a garret
Read books as though he broke up flints. Some met
In back rooms with hot red plush hangings,
And all outside the snow of foreign tongues.
One, a poet, went babbling like a fountain
Through parks. All were jokes to children.
All had the pale unshaven stare of shuttered plants
Exposed to a too violent sun.
Now all these
Drink their just praise from cups of waves;
And the translucent magnifying lights
Purify the achievement of their lives
With human bodies as words in history
Penned by their wills.

Their deeds and deaths are birds. They stop the invisible
Speed of our vacant sight across the sky.
In the past-coloured pigment of the mind's eye
They feed and fly and dwell.

Their time and land are death, since all
States and stays and makes
Them one with what they willed. We, who are living,
        seem
Exiles from them, more living: for we endure
Perpetual winter, waiting
Spring that will break our hardness into flowers
To set against their just and summer skies.

Our bodies are the pig and molten metal
Which theirs were once, before death cast
Their wills into those signatory moulds. . . .

Yet in the fluid past simplicity
Of those who now return
To greet us and advise us and to warn
Not giving us their love, but as examples,
Where do we recognize
Their similarity
To our own wandering present uncertainty?

What miracle divides
Our purpose from our weakness? What selects
Our waking from our sleeping and our acts
From madness? Who recognizes
Our image by the head and balanced eyes
And forming hands, and not the hidden shames?

Who carves
Our will and day and acts as history
And our likeness into statues
That walk in groves with those who went before?

How are we justified?

O utter with your tongues
Of angels, fire your guns—O save and praise—
Recall me from life's exile, let me join
Those who now kneel to kiss their sands,
And let my words restore
Their printed, laurelled, victoried message.

THE PAST VALUES

Alas for the sad standards
In the eyes of the old masters
Sprouting through glaze of their pictures!

For what we stare at through glass
Opens on to our running time:
As nature spilled before the summer mansion
Pours through windows in on our dimension.

And the propeller's rigid transparent flicker
To airman over continental ranges
Between him and the towns and river
Spells dynamics of this rotating
Age of invention, too rapid for sight.

Varnish over paint and dust across glass:
Stare back, remote, the static drum;
The locked ripeness of the Centaurs' feast;
The blowing flags, frozen stiff
In a cracked fog, and the facing
Reproach of self-portraits.

Alas for the sad standards
In the eyes of the freshly dead young
Sprawled in the mud of battle.
Stare back, stare back, with dust over glazed
Eyes, their gaze at partridges,
Their dreams of girls, and their collected
Faith in home, wound up like a little watch.

To ram them outside time, violence
Of wills that ride the cresting day
Struck them with lead so swift
Their falling sight stared through its glass.
Our sight stares back on death, like glass
Infringing the rigid eyes with toneless glaze,
Sinking stretched bodies inch-deep in their frames.

Through glass their eyes meet ours
Like standards of the masters
That shock us with their peace.

AN ELEMENTARY SCHOOL CLASS ROOM IN A SLUM

Far far from gusty waves, these children's faces.
Like rootless weeds the torn hair round their paleness.
The tall girl with her weighed-down head. The paper-
    seeming boy with rat's eyes. The stunted unlucky heir
Of twisted bones, reciting a father's gnarled disease,
His lesson from his desk. At back of the dim class,
One unnoted, sweet and young: his eyes live in a dream
Of squirrels' game, in tree room, other than this.

On sour cream walls, donations. Shakespeare's head
Cloudless at dawn, civilized dome riding all cities.
Belled, flowery, Tyrolese valley. Open-handed map
Awarding the world its world. And yet, for these
Children, these windows, not this world, are world,
Where all their future's painted with a fog,
A narrow street sealed in with a lead sky,
Far far from rivers, capes, and stars of words.

Surely Shakespeare is wicked, the map a bad example
With ships and sun and love tempting them to steal—
For lives that slyly turn in their cramped holes
From fog to endless night? On their slag heap, these
    children
Wear skins peeped through by bones and spectacles of
    steel
With mended glass, like bottle bits on stones.
All of their time and space are foggy slum
So blot their maps with slums as big as doom.

Unless, governor, teacher, inspector, visitor,
This map becomes their window and these windows
That open on their lives like crouching tombs
Break, O break open, till they break the town
And show the children to the fields and all their world
Azure on their sands, to let their tongues
Run naked into books, the white and green leaves open
The history theirs whose language is the sun.

THE UNCREATING CHAOS

I

To the hanging despair of eyes in the street, offer
Your making hands and your guts on skewers of pity.
When the pyramid sky is piled with clouds of sand which
    the yellow
Sun blasts above, respond to that day's doom
With a headache. Let your ghost follow
The young men to the Pole, up Everest, to war: by love,
    be shot.

For the uncreating chaos descends
And claims you in marriage: though a man, you were ever
    a bride:
Ever beneath the supple surface of summer muscle,
The fountain evening talk cupping the summer stars,
The student who chucks back the lock from his hair in
    front of a silver glass,
You were only anxious that all these passions should last.

The engine in you, anxiety,
Was a grave lecher, a globe-trotter, one
Whose moods were straws, the winds that puffed them,
    aeroplanes.
'Whatever happens, I shall never be alone,
I shall always have an affair, a railway fare, or a revolu-
    tion.'
Without your buttressing gesture that yet so leans;
Is glad as a mat
When stamped on; blood that gives suck to a vampire
    bat;

And your heart fretted by winds like rocks at Land's
    End:
You'd stand alone in a silence that never uttered
And stare in yourself as though on a desolate room.

II

I stand so close to you,
I will confess to you.
At night I'm flooded by a sense of future,
The bursting tide of an unharnessed power
Drowning the contours of the present.

In thoughts where pity is the same as cruelty,
Your life and mine seem water. Whether
What flows and wavers is myself
Or my thought streaming over you—or over all
The town and time—we are the same.
But beyond windows of this waking dream
Facts do their hundred miles an hour
Snorting in circles round the plain;
The bikes and track are real; and yet the riders lose
All sense of place; they're ridden by
Their speed; the men are the machines.

All I can warn you now—more I shall learn—
Is that our fear makes all its opposite.
Your peace bursts into war.
You're coined into a savage when you flee
The splitting crystal civilization dangles.
And when you choose a lover like a mirror
You see yourself reflected as a gunman.

You are a ghost amongst the flares of guns
Less living than
The shattered dead whose veins of mineral
We mine for here.
                    Alter your life.

III

Dissection of Empires, multiplication of crowns
By secret Treaty. But the pigeons scatter
Above the pavement at the fatal shot.
Heads bounce down stone steps.

Meagre men shoot up. Rockets, rockets,
A corporal's fiery tongue wags above burning parliament.
There flows in the tide of killers, the whip-masters,
Breeches and gaiters camouflage blood.

O visions of a faltering will
Inventing violent patterns!

History rushes. The crowds in towns,
Cerebral boundaries of nations over mountains,
Actors in flesh and death and material nature,
Dance to a gripless private stammer of shouting
. . . . Thoughts in a dying minister's brain.

IV

Shall I never reach
The field guarded by stones
Precious in the stone mountains,
Where the scytheless wind

Flushes the warm grasses:
Where clouds without rain
Add to the sun
Their lucid sailing shine?
The simple mechanism is here,
Clear day, thoughts of the work-room, the desk,
The hand, symbols of power.
Here the veins may pour
Into the deed, as the field
Into the standing corn.
Meanwhile, where nothing's pious
And like no longer willed,
Nor the human will conscious,
Holy is lucidity
And the mind that dare explain.

PART TWO

HOELDERLIN'S OLD AGE

When I was young I woke gladly in the morning
With the dew I grieved towards the close of day.
Now when I rise I curse the white cascade
That refreshes all roots, and I wish my eyelids
Were dead shutters pushed down by the endless weight
Of a mineral world. How strange it is that at evening
When prolonged shadows lie down like cut hay
In my mad age I rejoice and my soul sings
Burning vividly in the centre of a cold sky.

HAMPSTEAD AUTUMN

In the fat autumn evening street
Hands from my childhood stretch out
And ring muffin bells. The Hampstead
Incandescence burns behind windows
With talk and gold warmth.
Those brothers who we were lie wrapped in flannel,
And how like a vase looks my time then
Rounded with meals laid on by servants
With reading alone in a high room and looking down on
The pleasures of the spoiled pets in the garden—
A vase now broken into fragments,
Little walks which quickly reach their ends,
The islands in the traffic. To questions—I know not
    what——
Answers hurry back from the world,
But now I reject them all.
I assemble an evening with space
Pinned above the four walls of the garden,
A glowing smell of being under canvas,
The sunset tall above the chimneys,
From behind the smoke-screen of poplar leaves
A piano cutting out its images,
Continuous and fragile as china.

IN THE STREET

After the lies and lights of the complex street
Cat-calls of vice, virtue's conceit, I shall be glad to greet
A blank wall with my self face to face
And between the intricate stones no speaking lip of ex-
    cuse.

THE ROOM ABOVE THE SQUARE

The light in the window seemed perpetual
Where you stayed in the high room for me;
It flowered above the trees through leaves
Like my certainty.

The light is fallen and you are hidden
In sunbright peninsulas of the sword:
Torn like leaves through Europe is the peace
Which through me flowed.

Now I climb alone to the dark room
Which hangs above the square
Where among stones and roots the other
Peaceful lovers are.

THE MARGINAL FIELD

On the chalk cliff edge struggles the final field
Of barley smutted with tares and marbled
With veins of rusted poppy as though the plough had
    bled.
The sun is drowned in bird-wailing mist,
The sea and sky meet outside distinction,
The landscape glares and stares—white poverty
Of gaslight diffused through frosted glass.

This field was the farmer's extremest thought
And its flinty heart became his heart
When he drove below the return it yields
The wage of the labourer sheeted in sweat.
Here the price and the cost cross on a chart
At a point fixed on the margin of profit
Which opens out in the golden fields

Waving their grasses and virile beards
On the laps of the dripping valleys and flushing
Their pulsing ears against negative skies.
Their roots clutch into the flesh of the soil,
As they fall to the scythe they whisper of excess
Heaped high above the flat wavering scale
Near the sea, beyond the wind-scarred hill

Where loss is exactly equalled by gain
And the roots and the sinews wrestle with stone
On the margin of what can just be done
To eat back from the land the man the land eats.
Starved outpost of wealth and final soldier,
Your stretched-out bones are the frontier of power
With your mouth wide open to drink in lead.

A FOOTNOTE

(from Marx's Chapter on The Working Day)

"Heard say that four times four is eight,
"And the king is the man what has all the gold."
"Our king is a queen and her son's a princess
"And they live in a palace called London, I'm told."

"Heard say that a man called God who's a dog
"Made the world with us in it," "And then I've heard
"There came a great flood and the world was all
      drownded
"Except for one man, and he was a bird."

"So perhaps all the people are dead, and we're birds
"Shut in steel cages by the devil who's good,
"Like the miners in their pit cages
"And us in our chimneys to climb, as we should."

—Ah, twittering voices
Of children crawling on their knees
Through notes of Blue Books, History Books,
At foot of the most crowded pages,
You are the birds of a songless age
Young like the youngest gods, rewarded
With childhood that for ever stays.
Stunted spirits in a fog
Woven over the whole land
Into brown tapestries,
You cry among the wheels and endless days
To your stripped and holy mothers
With straps tied around their waists

For dragging trucks along a line.
In the sunset above these towns
Often I watch you lean upon the clouds
Momently drawn back like a curtain
Revealing a serene, waiting eye
Above a tragic, ignorant age.

THOUGHTS DURING AN AIR RAID

Of course, the entire effort is to put myself
Outside the ordinary range
Of what are called statistics. A hundred are killed
In the outer suburbs. Well, well, I carry on.
So long as the great 'I' is propped upon
This girdered bed which seems more like a hearse,
In the hotel bedroom with flowering wallpaper
Which rings in wreathes above, I can ignore
The pressure of those names under my fingers
Heavy and black as I rustle the paper,
The wireless wail in the lounge margin.
Yet supposing that a bomb should dive
Its nose right through this bed, with me upon it?
The thought is obscene. Still, there are many
To whom my death would only be a name,
One figure in a column. The essential is
That all the 'I's should remain separate
Propped up under flowers, and no one suffer
For his neighbour. Then horror is postponed
For everyone until it settles on him
And drags him to that incommunicable grief
Which is all mystery or nothing.

VIEW FROM A TRAIN

The face of the landscape is a mask
Of bone and iron lines where time
Has ploughed its character.
I look and look to read a sign,
Through errors of light and eyes of water
Beneath the land's will, of a fear
And the memory of chaos,
As man behind his mask still wears a child.

THE MIDLANDS EXPRESS

Muscular virtuoso!
Once again you take the centre of the stage,
The flat Midlands.
The signals are all down, the curtain is raised
As with unerring power you drive
Straight to your goal.
You pull down all the Northern iron-rifted
Mountains to your knees,
Until they're pressed beneath your feet
Dragging my sight back with their weight.
You drive the landscape like a herd of clouds
Moving against your horizontal tower
Of steadfast speed.
All England lies beneath you like a woman
With limbs ravished
By one glance carrying all these eyes.
O juggler of the wheeling towns and stars
Unpausing even with the night,
Beneath my lines I read your iron lines
Like the great art beneath a little life
Whose giant travelling ease
Is the vessel of its effort and fatigue.

THE INDIFFERENT ONE

I take the lift to the eighth floor,
Walk through the steam of corridors
And knock at the numbered door.
Entering the porch, I pass
My face reflected palely in a glass,
Lean, with hollows under the eyes,
A heightened expression of surprise,
Skin porous, like cells in a hive,
And I think: 'Can you forgive?'

Yes, you accept. On the thin bed
Above the city night we float
Embodied on the waves, their boats,
Arm locked in arm, head against head,
Whilst the nerves' implicit contacts
Through the hidden cables spark.
All dips and enters and forgets in dark
Except my single staring sight
Hanging above its pilot light.

Upturned to the unwritten ceiling
My eyes there read another you,
The naked human figure leaning
With one hand raised towards a view
Between whose hills are the blue spaces,
Perspective of my happiness!
There on your lips the clear light lives
Diffusing with its equable waves
The smile's indifference which forgives.

THREE DAYS

Our three long and spacious days
Rounded with their summer skies
Above the sea among
The islands of the hills, where, standing
Upon the morning's tufted height, we saw
Across the valleys of the afternoon, our distant
Goal of evening resting on a point
Stretched into the waves,
Are dropped like unknown lives in oceans
To complete their oblivion—
Spiral journeys to happiness made short
As a past or passing thought.

What can I do, now I return, to hold
Against the present their little memory?
From the rhythm of the country-drinking body
What muscle asserts happiness against
The anxiety of the city?
What words we spoke sustain their singing birds
Against the printed flood of words?
What peace we gave each other signs
Away the storm of wars?
There swims within my life a fish
Which is the deep and glittering wish
Evoking all the hills and waters
Of sensual memories.
Your image and those days of glass
Being lost become no loss
But change into that image
At the centre of my thought,
Itself no less precious
Than the original happiness.

PART THREE

TWO ARMIES

Deep in the winter plain, two armies
Dig their machinery, to destroy each other.
Men freeze and hunger. No one is given leave
On either side, except the dead, and wounded.
These have their leave; while new battalions wait
On time at last to bring them violent peace.

All have become so nervous and so cold
That each man hates the cause and distant words
Which brought him here, more terribly than bullets.
Once a boy hummed a popular marching song,
Once a novice hand flapped the salute;
The voice was choked, the lifted hand fell,
Shot through the wrist by those of his own side.

From their numb harvest all would flee, except
For discipline drilled once in an iron school
Which holds them at the point of a revolver.
Yet when they sleep, the images of home
Ride wishing horses of escape
Which herd the plain in a mass unspoken poem.

Finally, they cease to hate: for although hate
Bursts from the air and whips the earth like hail
Or pours it up in fountains to marvel at,
And although hundreds fall, who can connect

The inexhaustible anger of the guns
With the dumb patience of these tormented animals?

Clean silence drops at night when a little walk
Divides the sleeping armies, each
Huddled in linen woven by remote hands.
When the machines are stilled, a common suffering
Whitens the air with breath and makes both one
As though these enemies slept in each other's arms.

Only the lucid friend to aerial raiders,
The brilliant pilot moon, stares down
Upon the plain she makes a shining bone
Cut by the shadow of many thousand bones.
Where amber clouds scatter on no-man's-land
She regards death and time throw up
The furious words and minerals which kill life.

ULTIMA RATIO REGUM

The guns spell money's ultimate reason
In letters of lead on the spring hillside.
But the boy lying dead under the olive trees
Was too young and too silly
To have been notable to their important eye.
He was a better target for a kiss.

When he lived, tall factory hooters never summoned him.
Nor did restaurant plate-glass doors revolve to wave him
   in.
His name never appeared in the papers.
The world maintained its traditional wall
Round the dead with their gold sunk deep as a well,
Whilst his life, intangible as a Stock Exchange rumour,
   drifted outside.

O too lightly he threw down his cap
One day when the breeze threw petals from the trees.
The unflowering wall sprouted with guns,
Machine-gun anger quickly scythed the grasses;
Flags and leaves fell from hands and branches;
The tweed cap rotted in the nettles.

Consider his life which was valueless
In terms of employment, hotel ledgers, news files.
Consider. One bullet in ten thousand kills a man.
Ask. Was so much expenditure justified
On the death of one so young and so silly
Lying under the olive trees, O world, O death?

THE COWARD

Under the olive trees, from the ground
Grows this flower, which is a wound.
It is easier to ignore
Than the heroes' sunset fire
Of death plunged in their willed desire
Raging with flags on the world's shore.
Its opened petals have no name
Except the coward's nameless shame
Whose inexpiable blood
For his unhealing wound is food.
A man was killed, not like a soldier
With lead but with rings of terror;
To him, that instant was the birth
Of the final hidden truth
When the troopship at the quay,
The mother's care, the lover's kiss,
The following handkerchiefs of spray,
All led to the bullet and to this.
Flesh, bone, muscle and eyes
Assembled in a tower of lies
Were scattered on an icy breeze
When the deceiving past betrayed
All their perceptions in one instant,
And his true gaze, the sum of present,
Saw his guts lie beneath the trees.

Lest every eye should look and see
The answer to its life as he,
When the flesh prizes are all lost
In that white second of the ghost

Who grasps his world of loneliness
Sliding into empty space:—
I gather all my life and pour
Out its love and comfort here.
To populate his loneliness,
And to bring his ghost release,
My love and pity shall not cease
For a lifetime at least.

A STOPWATCH
AND AN ORDNANCE MAP

A stopwatch and an ordnance map.
At five a man fell to the ground
And the watch flew off his wrist
Like a moon struck from the earth
Marking a blank time that stares
On the tides of change beneath.
All under the olive trees.

A stopwatch and an ordnance map.
He stayed faithfully in that place
From his living comrade split
By dividers of the bullet
That opened wide the distances
Of his final loneliness.
All under the olive trees.

A stopwatch and an ordnance map.
And the bones are fixed at five
Under the moon's timelessness;
But another who lives on
Wears within his heart for ever
The space split open by the bullet.
All under the olive trees.

WAR PHOTOGRAPH

Where the sun strikes the rock and
The rock plants its shadowed foot
And the breeze distracts the grass and fern frond,

There, in the frond, the instant lurks
With its metal fang planned for my heart
When the finger tugs and the clock strikes.

I am that numeral which the sun regards,
The flat and severed second on which time looks,
My corpse a photograph taken by fate;

Where inch and instant cross, I shall remain
As faithful to the vanished moment's violence
As love fixed to one day in vain.

Only the world changes, and time its tense,
Against the creeping inches of whose moon
I launch my wooden continual present.

The grass will grow its summer beard and beams
Of light melt down the waxen slumber
Where soldiers lie dead in an iron dream;

My corpse be covered with the snows' December
And roots push through skin's silent drum
When the years and fields forget, but the whitened bones
     remember.

SONNET

The world wears your image on the surface
And judges, as always, the looks and the behaviour
Moving upon the social glass of silver;
But I plunged through those mirrored rays
Where eye remarks eye from the outside,
Into your hidden inner self and bore
As my self-love your hopes and failure,
The other self for which my self would have died.

Drowned in your life, I there encountered death
Which claimed you for a greater history
Where the free win, though many win too late.
We being afraid, I made my hand a path
Into this separate peace which is no victory
Nor general peace, but our escape from fate.

FALL OF A CITY

All the posters on the walls
All the leaflets in the streets
Are mutilated, destroyed or run in rain,
Their words blotted out with tears,
Skins peeling from their bodies
In the victorious hurricane.

All the names of heroes in the hall
Where the feet thundered and the bronze throats roared,
Fox and Lorca claimed as history on the walls,
Are now angrily deleted
Or to dust surrender their dust,
From golden praise excluded.

All the badges and salutes
Torn from lapels and from hands
Are thrown away with human sacks they wore
Or in the deepest bed of mind
They are washed over with a smile
Which launches the victors when they win.

All the lessons learned, unlearnt;
They young, who learned to read, now blind
Their eyes with an archaic film;
The peasant relapses to a stumbling tune
Following the donkey's bray;
These only remember to forget.

But somewhere some word presses
On the high door of a skull, and in some corner

Of an irrefrangible eye
Some old man's memory jumps to a child
—Spark from the days of energy.
And the child hoards it like a bitter toy.

AT CASTELLON

Backed to the brown walls of the square
The lightless lorry headlamps stare
With glinting reflectors through the night
At our gliding star of light.

Houses are tombs, tarpaulins cover
Mysterious trucks of the lorries over.
The town vacantly seems to wait
The explosion of a fate.

Our cigarettes and talking stir
Beneath the walls a small false ember.
A sentry stops us at his hut
Stamping with his rifle-butt.

Beside him stands a working man
With cheeks where suns have run.
'Take this comrade to the next village.'
The lines ploughed with ravage

Lift to a smile, the eyes gleam
And then relapse into their dream.
Head bent, he shuffles forward
And in without a word.

The car moves on to suns and time
Of safety for us and him.
But behind us on the road
The winged black roaring fates unload

Cargoes of iron and of fire
To delete with blood and ire
The will of those who dared to move
From the furrow, their life's groove.

THE BOMBED HAPPINESS

Children, who extend their smile of crystal,
And their leaping gold embrace,
And wear their happiness as a frank jewel,
Are forced in the mould of the groaning bull
And engraved with lines on the face.

Their harlequin-striped flesh,
Their blood twisted in rivers of song,
Their flashing, trustful emptiness,
Are trampled by an outer heart that pressed
From the sky right through the coral breast
And kissed the heart and burst.

This timed, exploding heart that breaks
The loved and little hearts, is also one
Splintered through the lungs and wombs
And fragments of squares in the sun,
And crushing the floating, sleeping babe
Into a deeper sleep.

Its victoried drumming enters
Above the limbs of bombed laughter
The body of an expanding State
And throbs there and makes it great,

But nothing nothing can recall
Gaiety buried under these dead years,
Sweet jester and young playing fool
Whose toy was human happiness.

PORT BOU

As a child holds a pet
Arms clutching but with hands that do not join
And the coiled animal watches the gap
To outer freedom in animal air,
So the earth-and-rock flesh arms of this harbour
Embrace but do not enclose the sea
Which, through a gap, vibrates to the open sea
Where ships and dolphins swim and above is the sun.
In the bright winter sunlight I sit on the stone parapet
Of a bridge; my circling arms rest on a newspaper
Empty in my mind as the glittering stone
Because I search for an image
And seeing an image I count out the coined words
To remember the childish headlands of this harbour.
A lorry halts beside me with creaking brakes
And I look up at warm waving flag-like faces
Of militiamen staring down at my French newspaper.
'How do they speak of our struggle, over the frontier?'
I hold out the paper, but they refuse,
They did not ask for anything so precious
But only for friendly words and to offer me cigarettes.
In their smiling faces the war finds peace, the famished
      mouths
Of the rusty carbines brush against their trousers
Almost as fragilely as reeds;
And wrapped in a cloth—old mother in a shawl—
The terrible machine-gun rests.
They shout, salute back as the truck jerks forward
Over the vigorous hill, beyond the headland.
An old man passes, his running mouth,

With three teeth like bullets, spits out 'pom-pom-pom'.
The children run after; and, more slowly, the women
Clutching their clothes, follow over the hill;
Till the village is empty, for the firing practice,
And I am left alone on the bridge at the exact centre
Where the cleaving river trickles like saliva.
At the exact centre, solitary as a target,
Where nothing moves against a background of cardboard
    houses
Except the disgraceful skirring dogs; and the firing be-
    gins,
Across the harbour mouth from headland to headland,
White flecks of foam gashed by lead in the sea;
And the echo trails over its iron lash
Whipping the flanks of the surrounding hills.
My circling arms rest on the newspaper,
My mind seems paper where dust and ink fall,
I tell myself the shooting is only for practice,
And my body seems a cloth which the machine-gun
    stitches
Like a sewing machine, neatly, with cotton from a reel;
And the solitary, irregular, thin 'paffs' from the carbines
Draw on long needles white threads through my navel.

PART FOUR

DARKNESS AND LIGHT

To break out of the chaos of my darkness
Into a lucid day is all my will.
My words like eyes in night, stare to reach
A centre for their light: and my acts thrown
To distant places by impatient violence
Yet lock together to mould a path of stone
Out of my darkness into a lucid day.

Yet, equally, to avoid that lucid day
And to preserve my darkness, is all my will.
My words like eyes that flinch from light, refuse
And shut upon obscurity; my acts
Cast to their opposites by impatient violence
Break up the sequent path; they fly
On a circumference to avoid the centre.

To break out of my darkness towards the centre
Illumines my own weakness, when I fail;
The iron arc of the avoiding journey
Curves back upon my weakness at the end;
Whether the faint light spark against my face
Or in the dark my sight hide from my sight,
Centre and circumference are both my weakness.

O strange identity of my will and weakness!
Terrible wave white with the seething word!

Terrible flight through the revolving darkness!
Dreaded light that hunts my profile!
Dreaded night covering me in fears!
My will behind my weakness silhouettes
My territories of fear, with a great sun.

I grow towards the acceptance of that sun
Which hews the day from night. The light
Runs from the dark, the dark from light
Towards a black or white of total emptiness.
The world, my body, binds the dark and light
Together, reconciles and separates
In lucid day the chaos of my darkness.

THE HUMAN SITUATION

This I is one of
The human machines
So common on the grey plains—
Yet being built into flesh
My single pair of eyes
Contain the universe they see;
Their mirrored multiplicity
Is packed into a hollow body
Where I reflect the many, in my one.

The traffic of the street
Roars through my head, as in the genitals
Their unborn London.

And if this I were destroyed,
The image shattered,
My perceived, rent world would fly
In an explosion of final judgement
To the ends of the sky,
The colour in the iris of the eye.

Opening, my eyes say 'Let there be light',
Closing, they shut me in a coffin.
To perform the humming of my day,
Like the world, I shut the other
Stars out from my sky.
All but one star, my sun,
My womanly companion,
Revolving round me with light
Eyes that shine upon my profile
While the other profile lies in night.

My body looms as near me as, to the world,
The world. Eyelashes
Are reeds fringing a pond
Which shut out the moon.
Ranges, vertebrae, hair, skin, seas.
Everything is itself, nothing a map.
What's inside my bowels and brain,
The Spring and the volcanoes,
Include all possibilities of development
Into an unpredictable future,
Full of invention, discovery, conversion, accident.

No one can track my past
On a chart of intersecting lines:
No fountain-pen is filled from the womb
As I from my mother's blood stream.
My history is my ancestry
Written in veins upon my body:
It is the childhood I forget
Spoken in words I mispronounce:
In a calligraphy of bones
I live out some hidden thought
Which my parents did forget.

Faces of others seem like stars
Obedient to symmetrical laws.
I stare at them as though into a glass,
And see the external face of glass,
My own staring mask of glass,
Tracked with lines of reflexes.
Eyes, lashes, lips, nostrils, brows.
The distant features move on wires
Fixed to their withheld characters.

O law-giving, white-bearded father,
O legendary heroes, sailing through dreams
Looking for land when all the world was sea
And sunrise, O bare-kneed captain of my first school,
O victors of history, angry or gentle exponents
Of the body as an instrument which cuts
A pattern on the time, O love
Surrounding my life with violet skies,

It is impossible for me to enter
The unattainable ease
Of him who is always right and my opponent,
Of those who climb the dawn with such flexible knees,
Of those who won the ideologic victories,
Of her whose easy loving turned to flowers
The forbidden and distorted natural powers;

Impossible to imagine, impossible to wish
The entrance into their symbolic being
Death to me and my way of perceiving
As much as if I became a stone;
Here I am forced on to my knees,
On to my real and own and only being
As into the fortress of my final weakness.

THE SEPARATION

When the night within whose deep
Our minds and bodies melt in love,
Instead of joining us, divides
With winds and seas that tear between
Our separated sleep—

Then to my lidless eyes that stare
Beyond my dark and climbing fears,
Your answering warm island lies
In the gilt wave of desire
Far as the day from here.

Here where I lie is the hot pit
Crowding on the mind with coal
And the will turned against it
Only drills new seams of darkness
Through the dark-surrounding whole.

Our vivid suns of happiness
Withered from summer, drop their flowers;
Hands of the longed, withheld tomorrow
Fold on the hands of yesterday
In double sorrow.

The present voices and the faces
Of strangers mirroring each other
In their foreign happiness,
Lay waste and populate my map
With meaningless names of places.

To bring me back to you, the earth
Must turn, the aeroplane
Must fly across the glittering spaces,
The clocks must run, the scenery change
From mountains into town.

Against a wheel I press my brain,
My blood roars through a night of wood
But my heart uncoils no shoot
From the centre of a silence
Of motionless violence.

And when we meet—the ribs will still
Divide the flesh-enfolding dream
And the winds and seas of time
Ruin the islands with their stream
However compassed be the will;

Unless within the turning night
Where we are ever separate,
Our eyes drink in each other's silence,
Unmeasuring patience
Threaded upon their secret light.

Shuttered by dark at the still centre
Of the world's circular terror,
O tender birth of life and mirror
Of lips, where love at last finds peace
Released from the will's error.

TWO KISSES

I wear your kiss like a feather
Laid upon my cheek
And I wander to the quay where the river
Suggests suggests

The dirt off all the streets
And the rotting feet of factories,
But the swans and boats and corks ride
The buoyant running waters
And the eye is carried by a tide

To the far shore and day-green spaces,
And the ear is gently belied
By sounds under dreams under the roar outside.
And then the heart in its white sailing pride

Launches among the swans and the stretched lights
Laid on the water, as on your cheek
The other kiss and my listening
Life, waiting for all your life to speak.

THE LITTLE COAT

The little coat embroidered with birds
Is irretrievably ruined.
We bought it in the Spring
And she stood upon a chair,
A blazing tree of birds;
I leaned my head against her breast
And all the birds seemed to sing
While I listened to that one heavy bird
Thudding at the centre of our happiness.

But everything is torn away,
The clothes which were young and gay
Lie like dolls in attics
When the children have grown and ceased to play;
Or they fall with Autumn leaves
When fashions are blown out on white sales
Before the models of another day.

That great bed on which there lies
The charming haunting animal
Is a torrent that carries away
All the nests and singing branches
Tangled among blocks of ice
Which were the springs of yesterday.

Unless our love has wiser ways
Than the swallow glancing on
The azure summer surface,
To go when the waves rise.
—O hold me in that solemn kiss

Where our lips are changed to eyes
And in the deep lens of their gaze
Smiles and tears grow side by side
From the loving stillness.

VARIATIONS ON MY LIFE

THE FIRST

To knock and enter
Knock and enter
The cloudless posthumous door
Where the slack guts are drawn into taut music
And there to sit and speak
With those who went before;

And to be justified
At last being at their side
To know I have no quality
Of ultimate inferiority
But bear on rounded shoulders the weight of my hu-
    manity;

To look down on my life
And see a life
Sociable puppet painted with a mouth
And to give the mouth a voice
That is not death
But its own truth confessing its own justice;
And to accept
My own weakness beyond dispute
Which is the strength I reject
Reaching back to the past with a dark root
Where earth and womb connect.

There is never enough air
There is never a wide enough space
There is never a white enough light
There is never a three-dimensional paper
Where the praise may loop like an aeroplane:

To knock and enter
Knock and enter
The room white as paper
With light falling on a white space
Through high windows of power
On hands resting on the controlling table,
Hands severed from the wrists
Moving only with the thoughts in fingers;

And to find release
From the continual headache
And the necessity of such long journeys;
The necessity of being alone
And the never being alone
Away from the lighted cities of the brain;

To touch and kiss
The gold horizon of the withheld wish;
To enter the flower of those who fructify
And fall and fade in the night full of desire;
To know the physical enduring secret
Strength whispers to the acrobat;

And to enter
The cold frigate voyaging to despair:
For this also is life, this also
Is the journey to the wonderful snow.

What hunger! And what distances!
Here is far more than coldness
That so illumines the whole surface!
Here is the crystal microscopic rose
That out of the frozen nerve grows.

Oh, but to ride on
The whole quivering human machine!
Less efficient than an aeroplane
Rather, a feathered, artificial bird
Which hardly flies but holds our lives
In all its love.
Oh to be taken by it, and to hold
My ear against its ever-female heart,
And to accept its fleas and all its sins,
To explore all its gifts
And nothing, nothing to refuse.

To say I love and I forgive
And that I know all that I hold;
Never to slide
Away among the drawing-rooms and hatred
From what it gives—
That is to walk in a sacred grove

And pluck the ripened voices with their ears
Bound into sheaves filled with the sun
Of summers that spoke and then went on;
And among them to place
My own posthumous voice
Which nothing does refuse
And only death denies.

VARIATIONS ON MY LIFE

... Or to return
To the first loved friend, you
Whose life seemed most unlike my own
As though you existed on an island
In seas of an archaic time,
Hidden under birdsong and olive trees,
With eyes chiselled to reflect the sky,
And behind the blue the clear flame,
And the hoarded quietness
Of summer at evening that surrounds a wood
Loaded with thunder,
Whose gentleness withholds the trigger
Night and tiger.

If I could return
And with a gained balance of happiness,
The scales of a golden success,
Smile and reassure you and undo the unhappiness
I wound around us then;
If I had a common Midas touch,
The fingers of an electric sign—
As I remember you stood once
In the tar-streaked drizzling street
With the light on your hair,
Smile painted by a day
Neither yours nor mine.

And if I could cease to demand,
As I asked then,
I know not what demonstrable favour
Nor what invented want,
For I have this to offer—
I was the sea, I was the island
Where the casqued heroic head
Lay and was remembered;
My innocent crystal mirrored your heart,
My mind was your legendary sky of love.

If I could accept
Myself in those in whose
Sweetness my life dissolves
And trust they could accept
Themselves in me; nor fear
Their expert quick disfavour
At the way I frown or hold my head;
Nor the smiling easy rivals
In whose faces the South winds blow,
And who become most serious
When the night and dance revolve.

O, then my body would enter
Its island and its summer
The questions find their answer
And my head its resting-place
Where the other heart lies
Washed by the seas of blood
Under the trees and clouds
And the healing sky
Of the breast's breathing space.

And I would know the peace
Of some distant frequent face
Seen in street or train,
Full of withheld promise,
Which out of rapid day
Enters the tunnel of my dream
Endowed with every wish
And then is dragged away
Into rapid day again.

NAPOLEON IN 1814

Your heart was loaded with its fate like lead
Pressing against the net of flesh: and those
Countries that crept back across the boundaries
Where you had forced open the arena
Of limelit France with your star at the centre,
Closed in on you, terrified no longer
At the diamond in your head
Which cut their lands and killed their men.

You were the last to see what they all saw
That you, the blinding one, were now the blind
The Man of Destiny, ill destined.

For, as your face grew older, there hung a lag
Like a double chin in your mind. The jaw
Had in its always forward thrust
Grown heavy. The bones now drove
Towards a bed. But to sleep there, the peace
Must sign with blood the sheets of Russian snow.

Your quicksilver declaiming eye
Had frozen to the stare of a straight line
Which only saw goals painted in its beam
And made an artificial darkness all around
Which thickened into Allies.

Before, you were the genius whom all envied
An image of the self-delighting child
On his mother rosily seizing all
Till he was buried in stiff clothes and ruled
By a dead will becoming his own will. In you

The Caesars tamed by dying, fired again
Their lives in the unlegendary sky
With all the vulgar violence of Today.
And secretly you were much loved by all
Whose eyes sailed deep into their mirrors
To see whether a mouth culled like a flower
Might burst into Napoleon.

Then suddenly you ceased to be the prayer
Of hidden self to self. You changed into that one
Whom all the world looks at from the outside:
The nurse's bogey and the dragon
With scaly flanks gaped at by villagers
Smashing the harvest with its lashing tail.
Even the brutes could not imagine
The monstrousness of being you.

Men spoke of you as Nature, and they made
A science of your moods.
Your way of always marching forward
To fight a battle, and still marching on,
Was known like winter and like winter
Answered with a numbness all around
On which the boughs of a charred Moscow hung
Offering no life or food.

Your fate became your Elba where you stood
Upon your armies like a voyaging rock.
The world broke round, deep in its anger, yet
Transparent to your sun, salt, barren, tugged
By hidden tides of power and gold,
And with a flattering tongue that finally drowned.

Your generals fell out of your head like hair,
The tinsel victories from your gleaming laurels,
And your face became a glass
Where all looked through on to your losses.
The statesmen you had overthrown
Sprouted again in their gold leaves
And watched you shrivel back into a man.
O your heart beat the drum out that was you

Yet it felt something put aside, perhaps
Your youth, perhaps your throne—that piece of wood.
O your body still was brass
Around a trumpet mouth. O, it could call
The Guards out of their graves; four hours,
Which lost you Paris, back from yesterday;
Or multiply the cannon balls,
Those genitals of death;
O if you stretched your arm, you'd stretch out France.

All your thoughts were pouring yesterdays
With blood and flags and smoke and men
To fill the hollows of today.
Being all memory, you forgot
The narrow shaves of time. But the lean world,
Famished by you, and eating back again
Upon your fall, in all its bones and hunger
Was—like the unemployed that stare
With eyes from the stone edges—avidly Tomorrow.

The kings of yesterday might still have saved
Your throne for you—because you were a king.
If one, touching your shoulder,

Could persuade you to measure
Your claims against your present power,
The stature of your body in a mirror,
And not against that superhuman shadow
Struck by the sunset across your empire.

Yes, if he took you to the glass
And said "Look". But you would not see a map,
Nor would you see yourself. You'd see
Yourself and fate; and those commands
That once were armies, as the lines on your face,
And ghostly as the history in men's brains.

The world had been your language which you wrote
In carnage and the rape of lands.
The lines on the white paper followed after,
In thin black letters, what your lines
Of men wrote on the world.
But now the armies had crumbled and the words

Had caught up all the deeds and left behind
You with the wreck of deeds, the empty words,
As though you'd learnt yourself by heart
And knew nothing but that great rhetoric
Once echoing the thunder of the field
But now hidden in the hollow bones.

Yet what you made the world was always you
In your own mind, and what you won
In lands, you wrote upon men's brains:
And now that all was lost, it sprang again
Where in your heart already, Waterloo
Purely persisted, like an echo.

THE MASK

Involved in my own entrails and a crust
Turning a pitted surface towards a space,
I am a world that watches through a sky
And is persuaded by mirrors
To regard its being as an external shell,
One of a universe of stars and faces.

My life confronts my life with eyes, the world
The world with lenses: and the self-image
Lifted in light against the lens
Stares back with my dumb wall of eyes:
The seen and seeing softly mutually strike
Their glass barrier that arrests the sight.

But the world's being hides in the volcanoes
And the foul history pressed into its core;
And to myself my being is my childhood
And passion and entrails and the roots of senses;
I'm pressed into the inside of a mask
At the back of love, the back of air, the back of light.

The other lives revolve around my sight
Scratching a distant eyelid like the stars;
My life, my world, scarcely believes they live;
They are the mirrors of the foreign masks
Stamped into shapes, obedient to their laws
Following a course till death completes their arc.

HOUSES AT EDGE
OF RAILWAY LINES

To rise up and step out
Of the lurid shrieking cinder
Travelling more miles than minutes to the hour,
Iron on iron through the iron night
And its iron full of fire;

To rise up and throw away its will
Straight as a Roman frown
Joining a town to another town,
Falling through the night in an age of bombs
And full of tender watching eyes

Fixed on floodlit thoughts in magazines
Or sinking to their stomachs full of plans
Or searching for hope on the horizon,
The beam of a lost dawn,
Or browsing on furnace fires of doom;

And without knocking to enter
The life that lies behind
The edges of drawn blinds,
A sun behind the clouds
Of slums, suburbs and farms
Where love fills rooms, as gold
Pours into a valid mould.

A woman takes down her hair
Electric in the room

And fills her linen night-gown
As the air fills a balloon;
And her lover does not ask
For the window of the stage
Which opens on the eyes
Of the star-gazing critics,
For their love rests in the furrows
Of her wrinkled brow,
Lying there, as a line
Is laid on earth by the plough.

And heat and untidy hair
And beads of sweat on the skin
And the accepted smells,
His eyes buried in her breasts
Like rough quartz in a mine,
Make a forgiveness
Within the turning night
Of trains and frosts outside,
So tall and rushing else.

TO A SPANISH POET

(for Manuel Altolaguirre)

You stared out of the window on the emptiness
Of a world exploding:
Stones and rubble thrown upwards in a fountain
Blasted sideways by the wind.
Every sensation except loneliness
Was drained out of your mind
By the lack of any motionless object the eye could find.
You were a child
Who sees for the first time things happen.

Then, stupidly, the sulphur stucco pigeon
Fixed to the gable above your ceiling
Swooped in a curve before the window
Uttering, as it seemed, a coo.
When you smiled,
Everything in the room was shattered;
Only you remained whole
In frozen wonder, as though you stared
At your image in the broken mirror
Where it had always been silverly carried.

Thus I see you
With astonishment whitening in your gaze
Which still retains in the black central irises
Laughing images
Of a man lost in the hills near Malaga
Having got out of his carriage
And spent a week following a partridge;
Or of that broken-hearted general
Who failed to breed a green-eyed bull.

[80]

Beyond the violet violence of the news,
The meaningless photographs of the stricken faces,
The weeping from entrails, the vomiting from eyes,
In all the peninsular places,
My imagination reads
The penny fear that you are dead.

Perhaps it is we who are unreal and dead,
We of a world that revolves, dissolves and explodes
While we lay the steadfast corpse under the ground
Just beneath the earth's lid,
And the flowering eyes grow upwards through the grave
As through a rectangular window
Seeing the stars become clear and more clear
In a sky like a sheet of glass,
Beyond these comedies of falling stone.

Your heart looks through the breaking body,
Like axle through the turning wheel,
With eyes of blood.
Unbroken heart,
You stare through my revolving bones
On the transparent rim of the dissolving world
Where all my side is opened
With ribs drawn back like springs to let you enter
And replace my heart that is more living and more cold.

Oh let the violent time
Cut eyes into my limbs
As the sky is pierced with stars that look upon
The map of pain,
For only when the terrible river
Of grief and indignation

Has poured through all my brain
Can I make from lamentation
A world of happiness,
And another constellation,
With your voice that still rejoices
In the centre of its night,
As, buried in this night,
The stars burn with their brilliant light.

Ruins and Visions

SONG

Stranger, you who hide my love
    In the curved cheek of a smile
And sleep with her upon a tongue
    Of soft lies which beguile,
        Your paradisal ecstasy
    Is justified is justified
By hunger of all beasts beneath
    The overhanging cloud,
        Who, to snatch quick pleasures run,
        Before their momentary sun
Be eclipsed by death.

Lightly, lightly from my sleep
    She stole, our vows of dew to break,
Upon a day of melting rain
    Another love to take;
        Her happy happy perfidy
    Was justified was justified
Since compulsive needs of sense
    Clamour to be satisfied
        And she was never one to miss
        The plausible happiness
Of a new experience.

I, who stand beneath a bitter
      Blasted tree, with the green life
Of summer joy cut from my side
      By that self-justifying knife,
            In my exiled misery
            Were justified were justified
If upon two lives I preyed
      Or punished with my suicide,
            Or murdered pity in my heart
            Or two other lives did part
To make the world pay what I paid.

Oh, but supposing that I climb
      Alone to a high room of clouds
Up a ladder of the time
And lie upon a bed alone
      And tear a feather from a wing
And listen to the world below
And write round my high paper walls
      Anything and everything
Which I know and do not know!

A SEPARATION

Yes. The will decided. But how can the heart decide,
Lying deep under the surface
Of the level reasons the eye sees—
How can the heart decide
To banish this loved face for ever?

The starry eyes on the fringe of darkness
To forgo? The light within the body's blindness?
To prove that these were lost in any case,
And accept the stumbling stumps of consolations,

When under sleep, under the day,
Under the world, under the bones,
The unturning changeless heart,
Burning in suns and snows of passion,
Makes its mad protestations
And breaks, with vows and declarations?

THE VASE OF TEARS

Tears pouring from this face of stone,
Angels from the heart, unhappiness
From some dream to yourself unknown—
Let me dry your eyes with these kisses.
I pour what comfort of ordinariness
I can; faint light upon your night alone.
And then we smother with caresses
Both our starved needs to atone.

Stone face creased with human tears: yet
Something in me gentle and delicate
Sees through those eyes an ocean of green water
And one by one the bitter drops collects
Into my heart, a glass vase which reflects
The world's grief weeping in its daughter.

THE DOUBLE SHAME

You must live through the time when everything hurts
When the space of the ripe, loaded afternoon
Expands to a landscape of white heat frozen
And trees are weighed down with hearts of stone
And green stares back where you stare alone,
And the walking eyes throw flinty comments
And the words which carry most knives are the blind
Phrases searching to be kind.

Solid and usual objects are ghosts
The furniture carries cargoes of memory,
The staircase has corners which remember
As fire blows red in gusty embers,
And each empty dress cuts out an image
In fur and evening and summer and gold
Of her who was different in each.

Pull down the blind and lie on the bed
And clasp the hour in the glass of one room
Against your mouth like a crystal doom.
Take up the book and look at the letters
Hieroglyphs on sand and as meaningless—
Here birds crossed once and cries were uttered
In a mist where sight and sound are blurred.

For the story of those who made mistakes
Of one whose happiness pierced like a star
Eludes and evades between sentences
And the letters break into eyes which read

What the blood is now writing in your head,
As though the characters sought for some clue
To their being so perfectly living and dead
In your story, worse than theirs, but true.

Set in the mind of their poet, they compare
Their tragic bliss with your trivial despair
And they have fingers which accuse
You of the double way of shame.
At first you did not love enough
And afterwards you loved too much
And you lacked the confidence to choose
And you have only yourself to blame.

THE JOURNEY

Upon what confident iron rails
   We seemed to move to the clear view
At the end of the line, where, without fail,
   My visions would come true.

There, where the sun melts the curved hills
   In one transparent wave against the skies,
I'd see your tender smile, more than your will,
   Shine through the coldness of your eyes.

Our harsh tongues of to-day would run in tears
   Back to this buried Now become the past.
In the cool shadows we'd unclasp our fears
   Transformed to love at last.

Oh, but then suddenly the line
   Swung onto another view
Barren with myself, and the blank pain
   Of the crammed world without you.

A HALL OF MIRRORS

Into a hall of mirrors
A hall of many mirrors
I enter,

Searching for that one face
Of innocence: amongst your many faces
Endlessly repeated in the empty spaces
Of your own eyes;
Suspended thinly on threads
Of your own self-admiring gaze.

At last, at last, when the light drops
From the glass tongues of praise,
In the dark your eyes are afraid,
Cowering at the bottom of a sad and lonely pit,
And your head like a doll's on your arm falls.

Yet a voice flowers from your sleep
And Venus throbs through your shut eyelids.
I search through a tunnel of past years
For a child who stands quite alone
Fallen from the care of the world's hands,
Exposed to all her fears,
Her face bright as a fruit with wet tears,
And I fall down shafts of love
Into the abyss of something human
Something lost when the long nights advance,
Hidden behind the hands of chance.

I search deep in the wells of weakness
And I read the innocence beyond the lie

The truth behind the evasive eye,
The terrible lost innocence
Fluttering faintly in a distant dance,
And the truth that stands, and begs forgiveness.

Till I drown, drawn down by my own mercy.

Somewhere in the night, above the branches
Restless with tongues of leaves over the square,
Where you and I and all
The false play-acting puppets are,
In a high room, hidden in the darkness,
There lies your heart, the truly good,
Swathed in the flesh where all roses unfold,
Warm in the nest which is the root of beds,
Surrounding me with love like all the stars
Blessing a birth with seed of fires,
O, waiting with an infinite gift
Which to refuse to search and find
Is to be cold and cruel and blind.

NO ORPHEUS, NO EURYDICE

Nipples of bullets, precipices,
Ropes, knives, all
Now would seem as gentle
As the far away kisses
Of her these days remove
—To the dervish of his mind
Lost to her love.

There where his thoughts alone
Dance round his walls,
They paint his pale darling
In a piteous attitude standing
Amongst blowing winds of space,
Dead, and waiting in sweet grace
For him to follow, when she calls.

For how can he believe
Her loss less than his?
"True it is that she did leave
Me for another's kiss;
Yet our lives did so entwine
That the blank space of my heart
Torn from hers apart,
Tore hers too from mine."

O, but if he started
Upon that long journey
Of the newly departed
Where one and all are born poor

Into death naked,
Like a slum Bank Holiday
Of bathers on a desolate shore;

If, with nerves strung to a harp,
He searched among the spirits there,
Looking and singing for his wife
To follow him back into life
Out of this dull leaden place,
He would never find there
Her cold, starry, wondering face.

For he is no Orpheus,
She no Eurydice.
She has truly packed and gone
To live with someone
Else, in pleasures of the sun,
Far from his kingdoms of despair
Here, there, or anywhere.

A WILD RACE

I

I know a wild race
Foreign to their own time
Estranged from their loved
And hating home place.

Inhabitants of dead languages,
They still live in intact quarters
Of cities and speeches.

From ashen parchment
And corroded stone
Their bearded thoughts
Are still outspoken,

Out of dust and bone
The broken unbroken.

For their teeth stamped words
Which still flash with eyes
Where, whiter than paper,
Their day dazzles libraries.

And they were as far
From their contemporaries
As the living to-day
From those are.

Far as the stars
Whose out-of-the-past light

Ravishes to-night's night
With their present-
piercing future.

II

Their unloved love
Luminous with words
Like a sun burned
Through the transparent body
Of their day's beauty
For which they yearned.

Their endless need
And their timeless gift
Lay on the light eyelids
Of their self-seeking
Feminine city
Like a reproach, weighed
With immortality.

The beloved, afraid,
Laughed, and betrayed.

III

But a girl to-day, dreaming
On her wave of time
With April clouds dawdling
Through the mirror of her eyes,
Lays down her book
And smiles and sighs
Lifting her empty head
Across the gulf of centuries:—

"O, if print put on flesh
And these words were whispers
From the lips of the poet
In the vase of my face,
Then this wave would be a river
Where my name would float for ever
And my flower never fade.

"O, I would understand
What his own time and land
Never knew: that his heart
Was torn apart
By loss large as a vulture: hence
The black fury of his dress
And his hair in disorder.

"O, I would take his hand
And his words would be my mirror
Where I saw my face for ever."
She thinks, turning from her lover
Whose need then hung above her
Like an eagle in the air.

And across the gulf of time
The cold terrible snow mountains
Saw his naked heart alone
And they knew him
And he knew them.

THE WAR GOD

Why cannot the one good
Benevolent feasible
Final dove descend?

And the wheat be divided?
And the soldiers sent home?
And the barriers torn down?
And the enemies forgiven?
And there be no retribution?

Because the conqueror
Is an instrument of power,
With merciless heart hammered
Out of former fear,
When to-day's vanquished
Destroyed his noble father,
Filling his cradle with anguish.

His irremediable victory
Chokes back sobbing anxiety
Lest children of the slain
(When the ripe ears grow high
To the sickles of his own
And the sun goes down)
Rise in iron morning
To stain with blood the sky
And avenge their fathers again.

[99]

His heart broke before
His raging splendour.
The virgins of prayer
Fumble vainly for that day
Buried under ruins,
Of his pride's greatest murder
When his heart which was a child
Asking and tender,
He hunted and killed.

The lost filled with lead
On the helpless field
May dream the pious reason
Of mercy, but also
Their eyes know what they did
In their own proud season,
Their dead teeth bite the earth
With semen of new hatred.

For the world is the world
And not the slain
Nor the slayer, forgive,
Nor do wild shores
Of passionate histories
Close on endless love;
Though hidden under seas
Of chafing despair,
Love's need does not cease.

TO POETS AND AIRMEN

(Dedicated to Michael Jones in his life, and now in his memory)

Thinkers and airmen—all such
   Friends and pilots upon the edge
Of the skies of the future—much
   You require a bullet's eye of courage
   To fly through this age.

The paper brows are winged and helmeted,
   The blind ankles bound to a white road
Streaming through a night of lead
   Where cities explode.
   Fates unload

Hatred burning, in small parcels,
   Outrage against social lies,
Hearts breaking against past refusals
   Of men to show small mercies
   To men. Now death replies
Releasing new, familiar devils.

And yet, before you throw away your childhood,
   With the lambs pasturing in flaxen hair,
   To plunge into this iron war,
Remember for a flash the wild good
   Drunkenness where
   You abandoned future care,

And then forget. Become what
   Things require. The expletive word.
   The all-night-long screeching metal bird.
And all of time shut down in one shot
   Of night, by a gun uttered.

THE AIR RAID ACROSS THE BAY

I

Above the dead flat sea
And watching rocks of black coast
Across the bay, the high
Searchlights probe the centre of the sky
Their ends fusing in cones of light
For a brilliant instant held up
Then shattered like a cup.

They rub white rules through leaden dark,
Projecting tall phantom
Masts with swaying derricks
Above the sea's broad level decks.

They slide triangles and parallels
Of experimental theorems,
Proving the hypothesis
Of death, on wasted surfaces
Of measureless blank distances.

II

But through their gliding light-streams,
   An invisible ragged sound
Moves, trailed by two distraught beams.
   A thudding falls from remote cones
And pink sequins wink from a shot-silk screen.

   Seeds of killing drop on cells of sleep
Which hug these promontories like dark-brown winkles.

Fingers pick away
Human minds from hollow skulls.

III

The shining ladders slant
Up to the god of war
Exalted on those golden stilts
And riding in his car
Of a destroying star.

But the waves clucking in the rocks
And the sacred standing corn
Brittle, and swaying with metallic clicks,
Their secret wealth lock
In an elemental magic
Of ripeness, which mocks
The nails through flesh torn.

WINTER AND SUMMER

Within my head, aches the perpetual winter
Of this violent time, where pleasures freeze.
My inner eye anticipates for ever
Looking through naked trees and running wheels
Onto a blank transparent sky
Leading to nothing; as though, through iron aims,
It was stared back at by the filmy surface
Of a lid covering its own despair.
Thus, when the summer breaks upon my face
With the outward shock of a green wave
Crested with leaves and creamy foam of flowers,
I think the luxurious lazy meadows
Are a deceiving canvas covering
With a balmy paint of leafy billows,
The furious volleys of charioteering power
Behind the sun, racing to destroy.
    When under light lawns, heavy in their soil,
I hear the groaning of the wasted lives
Of those who revolve unreflecting wheels,
    Alas, I prove that I am right,
For if my shadowed mind affirmed the light
It would return to those green, foolish years
When to live seemed to stand knee-deep in flowers:
There, winter was an indoor accident,
Where, with head pressed against the glass, I watched
The garden, falsified by snow,
Waiting to melt, and become real again.

IN MEMORIAM

The senseless drone of the dull machines in the sky
  In a chain extending the boundaries
    Of a distant invisible will,
  Weaves a net of sound in the darkness on high
  Drawing the senses up in one Eye
    From our tunnelled entombed bodies,
Where everything stops but the wishes that kill.

  Living now becomes withered like flowers
    In the boring burned city which has no use
      For us but as lives and deaths to fill
  With fury the guns blazing back on the powers
  That scorch our small plot of blasted hours:
    Death we cannot refuse
Where everything stops but the wishes that kill.

  Driven by intolerance and volted with lies,
    We melt down the whirring bodies of boys
      And their laughter distil
  To plough metal hatred through the skies
  And write with their burning eyes over cities
    Sure no green summer joys,
Where everything stops but the wishes that kill.

  Filled with swear words, laughter and fire,
    Soothed by the girl hands and clothed in my words,
      What, my fine feather-head, laughing lad Bill,
  Was your life, but a curveting arc of desire
  Ricochetting in flames on your own funeral pyre
    Instinctive as birds,
Where everything stops but the wishes that kill?

JUNE 1940

The early summer prepares its green feasts
In the garden, hot on the blossom of the peach,
Pressed close by bird song, crossed by bees,
Electrified with lizards; and the voices each to each

Speak, afloat on deck chairs. They say
How little they know of the battle far away
Different from the war in France in their day.

Beyond the hot red walls, the blowing
Of dust on dog roses in the hedges,
The meadows weighed with shadows, bringing
Youths with girls and bicycles, at evening
Round the War Memorials of villages;

Beyond the crisp sea, with lines
Engraved by winds and keels on glass dunes,
Perpetually moving and appearing still,
Tiring the eye with a permanent dance;
Far away! Divided by gleaming scissors
Of the steel channel—the raw edge of France.
Through their voices there moves a murmur like a ball
Rolled across the plains and hills,
Divided to ruffled whispers by the seas.

For the German caterpillar-wheeled dreams,
Imagined into steel, volley
Through the spring songs and the green hedges,
Crushing the lark's nest, with a roar of smoke,
Through the weak barriers of France.

"False is this feast which the summer, all one garden,
Spreads before the senses. Our minds must harden."

"Nor ears nor eyes, but the will
Is the perceiving organ of the soul.
Man's world is not nature, but Hell
Where he struggles to make a nightmare whole."

"History is a dragon under the soil
Wearing to-day only as a skin
Which man sloughs off when his dreams begin."

"The season of our soul is doom
Born to-day from a terrible womb."

"Yes, we see the dragon's teeth of the past
From a hungry childhood grown
Into avenging warriors at last."

"Indolent injustice for so long
Snoring over Germany, now is overthrown:
To face us with a still greater wrong."

"While we forgot, and the sun seemed to forgive,
Those bitter children were alive.
Their hatred never forgot to thrive."

"Well, well, the greater wrong must meet
To-morrow with a worse defeat."

Afloat on the lawn, the ghastly last-war voices
With blue eyes gaze for a moment on this:
England chained to the abyss.

Then, altogether, they begin
To murmur: "Of course, we shall win."

But the voice of one who was young and died
In a great battle, in the light leaves sighed:—

"I lay down with a greater doubt:
That it was all wrong from the start:
Victory and defeat both the same,
Hollow masks worn by shame
Over the questions of the heart.
And there was many another name
Dividing the sun's light like a prism
With the rainbow colours of an 'ism'.
I lay down dead like a world alone
In a sky without faith or aim
And nothing to believe in,
Yet an endless empty need to atone."

THE AMBITIOUS SON

Old man, with hair made of newspaper cutting
And the megaphone voice,
Dahlia in the public mind, strutting
Like a canary before a clapping noise,

My childhood went for rides on your wishes
As a beggar's eye strides a tinsel horse,
And how I reeled before your windy lashes
Fit to drive a paper boat off its course!

Deep in my heart I learned this lesson
As well have never been born at all
As live through life and fail to impress on
Time, our family name, inch-tall.

Father, how we both pitied those who had let
The emptiness of their unknown name
Gleam on a rose and fade on a secret,
Far from our trumpeting posthumous fame!

For how shall we prove that we really exist
Unless we hear, over and over,
Our ego through the world persist
With all the guns of the self-lover?

Oh, when the weight of Time's whole darkness
Presses upon our shuttered fall,

How shall we prove, if our lives went markless,
That we have lived at all?

But, my admired one, imagine my sorrow
When I watched the schoolboys' inquisitive faces
Turn away from your Day, and To-morrow
Mock your forehead with sneering grimaces.

Soon you lay in your grave like a crumpled clown
Eaten by worms, by quicklime forgotten,
Fake, untragic, pelted down
By a generation still more rotten.

When I left the funeral, my face was hard
With my contempt for your failure still
But, Father, my hardness was a scabbard
Sheathing your undefeated will.

Behold, a star fled from your breast
Of death, into my life of night
Making your long rest my unrest,
My head burn with frustrated light.

Through my breast there broke the fire
Of a prophetic son's anointment
Seeking a fame greater than Empire.
It was then I made my appointment

With Truth, beyond the doors of Death.
How like an engine do I press
Towards that terminus of my last breath,
When all the Future you and I possess

Will open out onto those endless spaces
Where, from an incorruptible mine,
Yours and my name take their places
Among the deathless names that shine!

O Father, to a grave of fame I faithfully follow!
And yet I love the glance of failure tilted up
With swimming eyes and waiting lips, to swallow
The sunset from the sky as from a cup.

Often I stand, as though outside a wall,
Outside a beggar's face, where a child seems hidden,
And I remember being lost, when I was small,
In a vast, deserted garden.

If I had the key I might return
To where the lovers lie forgotten on bright grass.
The prisoners and the homeless make me burn
With homesickness when I pass.

Yes! I could drown in lives of weakness,
For I pity and I understand
The wishes and fulfilments under the dream surface
Of an oblivious and uncharted land.

TOD UND DAS MAEDCHEN

From a tree choked by ivy, rotted
By liver-shaped fungus on the bark,
Out of a topmost branch
A single sprig is seen
That shoots against the sky its mark,
As though the dying trunk could launch
The whole life of the sap
Into one wedge-shaped steadfast glance
Above the lapping shining circling evergreen.

So with you,
Where you are lying,
The strong tide of your limbs drawn back
By green tides of regret,
And the sorrowful golden flesh
Scorched on by disease,
How difficult is dying
In your living dying eyes.

Oh how, when you have died,
Shall I remember to forget,
And with knives to separate
Your death from my life—
Since, darling, there is never a night
But the restored prime of your youth
Peaceful, does not float
Upon my sleep, as on a boat,
With the glance of love that lives
Inescapably as truth.

THE DROWNED

They still vibrate with the sound
Of electric bells,
The sailors who drown
While their mouths and ships fill
With wells of silence
And horizons of distance.

Kate and Mary were the city
Where they lingered on shore
To mingle with the beauty
Of the girls: they're still there—
Where no numbness nor dumbness
Appals dance hall and bar.

No letters reach wrecks;
Corpses have no telephone;
Cold tides cut the nerves
The desires are frozen
While the blurred sky
Rubs bitter medals on the eyes.

Jack sees her with another
And he knows how she smiles
At the light facile rival
Who so easily beguiles
Dancing and doing
What he never will now.

Cut off unfairly
By the doom of doom

Which makes heroes and serious
Skulls of men all,
Where under waves we roll
Whose one dream was to play
And forget death all day.

WINGS OF THE DOVE

Poor girl, inhabitant of a strange land
Where death shines through your gaze,
As though a terrible moonlight
Stared through these light days
With the skull-like gleam of night;

Poor child, you wear your summer dress
And your scarf striped with gold
As the earth wears a variegated cover
Of coloured flowers
Covering chaos and destruction over
Where deaths are told.

I look into your sunk eyes,
Shafts of wells to both our hearts,
Which cannot take part in the lies
Of acting these gay parts.
Under our lips, our minds
Become one with the weeping
Of the mortality
Which through sleep is unsleeping.

Of what use is my weeping?
It does not carry a surgeon's knife
To cut the wrongly multiplying cells
At the root of your life.
It can only prove
That extreme love
Stretches beyond the flesh to hideous bone
Howling in the dark alone.

Oh, but my grief is thought, a dream,
Which a clean gale will sweep away.
It does not wake every day
To the facts which are and do not merely seem:
The granite facts around your bed,
Poverty-stricken hopeless ugliness
Of the fact that you will soon be dead.

THE FATES

I

In the theatre,
The actors act the ritual of their parts,
Clowns, killers, lovers, captains,
At the end falling on the sword
Which opens out a window through their hearts
And through the darkness to the gleaming eyes
Of the watching masks slightly bored,

Of the audience
Acting the part of their indifference,
Pretending the thrusting pistons of the passions,
Contorted masks of tears and mockery,
Do not penetrate the surface fashions
Covering their own naked skins.

"We are not green fools nor black-eyed tragedians,
Though perhaps, long ago, we were the killers.
Still, still we have our moments of romance
Under the moon, when we are the lovers.
But the rules of fate do not apply to us.
The howling consequences can be bribed away
Discreetly, without fuss.
When we have left the play
The furies of atonement will not follow after
Our feet, into the street
Where the traffic is controlled all day."

Sitting in stalls or pit, they pray
That the externalized disaster

Gesticulating puppets display
Will not, with finger of catastrophe
Revolve on them its hissing frontal limelight:
Not lift the curtains of their windows,
Not rape their daughters in the coarse embrace
Of the promiscuous newspapers
Running with them in headlines through the streets.
In their lives, they have cut few capers
So death, they hope, will be discreet,
Raising a silk hat,
Dressed in black, with a smile for each tear, polite.

Oh which are the actors, which the audience?
Those who sit back with a tear, a smile, a sigh,
Where they deny deny deny?
Or those on the stage who rip open their ribs
Lift the lids from their skulls, tear the skin from their
        arms,
Revealing the secret corridors of dreams,
The salt savour of the passions,

The crushed hyacinths of corruption,
The opera-singing sexual organs:
And within all, as in a high room,
Filled with a vacuum containing infinite space,
The soul playing at being a gull by a lake,
Turning somersaults, immensely bored,
Whistling to itself, writing memoirs of God,
Forgetting
What time and the undertakers undertake?

Oh which are the actors, which the audience?
The actors, who simulate?

Or those who are, who watch the actors
Prove to them there is no fate?
Where then is the real performance
Which finally sweeps actors and audience
Into a black box at the end of the play?

Both, both, vowing the real is the unreal,
Are stared at by the silent stars
Of the comprehensive universe
Staging its play of passions in their hearts.
It carries them off at the end in a hearse.

II

O brave, powdered mask of weeded motherhood
For twenty years denying that the real
Was ever anything but the exceptional,
You were an excellent stage manager,
For your dear son's sake, of your theatre,
Family life, not sombre, but light:
"This is the play where nothing happens that can matter
Except that we are sensible healthy and bright."

Your problem was no easy one,
Somehow to spare your only son
From the gloomy brooding blue of his father's eyes,
After the War, for twenty years
Pacing the lawn between two wars,
His sombre way of staring at the table.
You were courageous and capable
Gaily you called these things his "moods".
Just "moods", "moods", like anything else,
A chair, the empty clanging of alarm bells.

You rebuilt the Georgian house with the old lawn,
And the kitchen garden surrounded by a wall,
And the servants in the servants' hall
Tidying the rooms downstairs at dawn;
And you bought a fishing rod, a pony and a gun
And gave these serious playthings to your son.

The fresh air and the scenery did the rest.
He ripened and his laughter floated on the lake,
A foretaste of the memories that now suggest
His photograph with the shirt open at the neck.
He came downstairs to dinner, "dressed".

Then your triumphant happiness bound cords
Around his silken glance into one bow.
Catching your husband's eye, your face spoke words
"This is the world, we've left the past below."

If a guest came, and in the course
Of conversation, spoke of "so-and-so's divorce",
Or else, "Poor Lady X, she died of cancer",
You had your fine frank answer,
Questioning him with vivid curiosity,
Poverty, adultery, disease, what strange monstrosity!
You smiled, perhaps, at your guest's eccentricity
Dragging such specimens out on your floor.

Your son grew up, and thought it all quite real.
Hunting, the family, the business man's ideal.
The poor and the unhappy had his sympathy.
They were exceptions made to prove his rule.
And yet he had his moments of uneasiness

When in the dazzling garden of his family
With the green sunlight tilted on your dress,
His body suddenly seemed an indecency,
A changeling smuggled to the wrong address.

Still, he got married. She was dull, of course.
But everything had turned out quite all right.
The bride sailed on the picture page in white
Arm linked in his, face squinting in the light.
Your son wore uniform. You, the mother-in-law
Who'd brought him up into a world at war,
At last felt tired. You wondered what he knew of life,
Whether enough to satisfy his wife.
Perhaps he'd learned from nature, or his horse.

III

Oh, but in vain
Do men bar themselves behind their doors
Within the well-appointed house
Painting, in designed acts, life as they would see it,
By the fireside, in the garden, round the table.

The storm rises,
The thunderbolt falls, and how feeble
Is the long tradition strengthened with reverence
Made sacred to respect by all appearance,
Or the most up-to-date steel-and-concrete
To withstand fate.

The walls fall, tearing down
The fragile life of the interior.

The cherishing fire in its grate
Consumes the house, grown to a monster,
As though the cat had turned into a tiger
Leaping out of a world become a jungle
To destroy its master.

The parents fall
Clutching with weak hands beams snapped like straw,
And the handsome only son,
Tanned leader of his village team,
Is shaken out of the soft folds
Of silk, spoiled life, as from a curtain.

He is thrown out onto a field abroad.
A whip of lead
Strikes a stain of blood from his pure forehead.
Into the dust he falls,
The virginal face carved from a mother's kisses
As though from sensitive ivory,
Staring up at the sun, the eyes at last made open.

AT NIGHT

During day's foursquare light
All is measured by eyes from the outside,
Windows look and classify the clothes
Walking upon their scaffolding of world.

But at night
Structures are melted in a soft pond
Of darkness, up to the stars.

Man's mind swims, full of lamps,
Among foundations of the epoch.
Clothes fade to the same curtains
As night draws over the blaze of flesh.

His heart—surrounded by money,
Loaded with a house, and hub-like
Centring spokes of fashionable change—
Grows dizzy at uncertainty,
At life longer than single lives,
At an opening out of spaces
Revealing stars more numerous
Than the overcrowded populace.

Every social attribute gained
Falls into the Milky Way.
The questions so long hidden

Behind the answers of the present
Rise from the superstitious past
Like ghosts from ruined palaces.

Into his hand of a single moment
There pour forgotten races
With eyes opening on plains like flowers,

And the unknown nations to come after,
Unthinkable as his own death dismissed
To the vanishing point of the future;

All are crushed into the bones of Now
Knit in his flesh of loneliness.

Oh, but his "I" might glide
Here into another such "I"
Invisible in nakedness;
His heart in the heart of darkness find,
Stretching from lonely birth to lonely
Death, like a mind behind the mind,
The image of his own loneliness,

The answering inconsolable cry
Of lost humanity,
Which the explicit day
Colours and covers and explains away.

THE BARN

Half-hidden by trees, the sheer roof of the barn
Is warped to a river of tiles
By currents of the sky's weather
Through long damp years.

Under the leaves, a great butterfly's wing
Seems its brilliant red, streaked with dark lines
Of lichen and rust, an underwing
Of winter leaves.

A sapling, with a jet of flaming
Foliage, cancels with its branches
The guttered lower base of the roof, reflecting
The tiles in a cup of green.

Under the crashing vault of sky,
At the side of the road flashing past
With a rumour of smoke and steel,
Hushed by whispers of leaves, and bird song,
The barn from its dark throat
Gurgitates with a gentle booming murmur.

This ghost of a noise suggests a gust
Caught in its rafters aloft long ago,
The turn of a winch, the wood of a wheel.

Tangled in the sound, as in a girl's hair
Is the enthusiastic scent
Of vivid yellow straw, lit by a sun-beam
Laden with motes, on the boards of a floor.

IN A GARDEN

Had I pen ink and paper,
I think that they could carry
The weight of all these roses,
These rocks and massive trees.

The hills weigh peacefully on my mind,
The grottoed skull encloses
Shifting lights and shade.
Soft on the flesh all the green scene reposes

But that the singing of those birds
Pressed to the hot wall of the sky,
Tears through the listening writing of the eye
To a space beyond words.

A CHILDHOOD

I am glad I met you on the edge
Of your barbarous childhood.

In what purity of pleasure
You danced alone like a peasant
For the stamping joy's own sake!

How, set in their sandy sockets,
Your clear truthful transparent eyes
Shone out of the black frozen landscape
Of those grey-clothed schoolboys!

How your shy hand offered
The total generosity
Of original unforewarned fearful trust,
In a world grown old in iron hatred!

I am glad to set down
The first and ultimate you,
Your inescapable soul. Although
It fade like a fading smile
Or light falling from faces
Which some grimmer preoccupation replaces.

This happens everywhere at every time:
Joy lacks the cause of joy,
Love the answering love,
And truth the objectless persistent loneliness,
As they grow older,
To become later what they were

In childhood earlier—
In a grown-up world of cheating compromises.

Childhood, its own flower,
Flushes from the grasses with no reason
Except the sky of that season.
But the grown desires need objects
And taste of these corrupts the tongue
And the natural need is scattered
Amongst satisfactions which satisfy
A debased need.

Yet all prayers are on the side of
Giving strength to innocence,
So I pray for nothing new,
I pray only, after such knowledge,
That you may have the strength to become you.

And I shall remember
You, who, being younger,
Will probably forget.

INTO LIFE

Aiming from clocks and space,
  O Man of Flesh, I hew
    Your features, blow on blow.
I cut away each surface
    To lay bare what I know—
Universe within you.

Shut close in your mind,
  You never quite will learn
    To see your life as whole.
Your mirrors are too blind;
  They have no eyes that turn
    From each age on your soul.

Your sense flies to each facet
  Striking from each hour;
    Now all heat, now all brain,
  All sex, sickness, power;
That severe line, when I place it,
    Seems nothing but pain.

Yet all experience, like stars
  (In distances of night,
    Their brilliant separate incidents
Divided by light-years)
  Hangs in your eyes the lights
    Of sustained co-existence.

What you were, you are,
  And what you will be, you are, too.

Born, you're dead; loving, are sad.
The years add, star by star,
The whole of life consuming you
In fires of good and bad.

THE COAST

These riding and ridden faces
Upon the wheels and tracks of trade,
With ruts where money runs; their talk
A metal traffic; bodies jolting trucks; their glances
Squinting six months ahead to count the profit,
Not a day beyond;
These in the streets, the dives, the shops, the City,

Inhabit this coast of rocks,
Poriferous stone expectorated on
By jellied spittle; rockpools lisping—
Blog, blah, fligger, fluck, fick, mallock.

Where the tide furls back shallow finny waves,
My swearing mates in their blue dungarees
Stand on the endless mud-flats reaching back
To their unscrupulous births. The sea
Will swill away the tag-ends of their names
With cards, and all that harbours do forget.

Would not, to open any door
Onto the star socketed in a skull,
Or through the domed night to the balanced scales,
Or following threads leading to faith
Sustained between two pairs of eyes:
Be false and frail as flowers
Crushed by iron machines of power?

Yet there are eyes which float upon the wreckage
Secretly clinging to a gleaming straw.

Some acts of kindness wave their handkerchiefs.
A trickling life runs through clogged veins
And streams flow backward buried under flesh.

A wind blows hither

Rest, rest, you ghoulish masks of life,
At last the fingers of the sky
Will lift the hard expressions from your tongues,
Unlock the mild sighs from your skulls,
Laugh with the laughter clinging to the marrow,
And knit you, flesh and bone,
Into a life of joy again.

DUSK

Steel edge of plough
Thrusts through the stiff
Ruffled fields of turfy
Cloud in the sky.
Above charcoal hedges
And dead leaf of land
It cuts out a deep
Gleaming furrow
Of clear glass looking
Through our funnelled day
Up a stair of stars.

On earth below
The knotted hands
Lay down their tasks,
And the wooden handles
Of steel implements
Gently touch the ground.
The shifting animals
Wrinkle their muzzles
At the sweet passing peace,
Like bells, of the breeze;
And the will of Man
Floats loose, released.

The dropping day
Encloses the universe
In a wider mantel
Than meridian blaze.
A terra cotta blanket

Of dark, robs one by one
Recognition from villages,
Features from flowers,
News from men,
Stones from the sun.

All the names fade away.
With a spasm, nakedness
Assumes menkind.
Their minds, cast adrift
On beds in upper rooms,
Awaiting the anchorage
Of sleep, see more
Than a landscape of words.

The great lost river
Crepitates
Through creeks of their brains.
Long-buried days
Rise in their dreams.
Their tight fists unclose
The powers they hold,
The manners and gold.

Then the burning eye
Of a timeless Being
Stares through their limbs
Drawing up through their bones
Mists of the past
Filled with chattering apes,
Bronze and stone gifts,
From all continents
Of the tree of Man.

The sun of this night
Mocks their dark day
Filled with brief aims
—Stealing from their kind
And killing their kind.
Abandoning hope,
They turn with a groan
From that terror of love
Back to their daybreak of
Habitual hatred.

DAYBREAK

At dawn she lay with her profile at that angle
Which, sleeping, seems the stone face of an angel;
Her hair a harp the hand of a breeze follows
To play, against the white cloud of the pillows.
Then in a flush of rose she woke, and her eyes were open
Swimming with blue through the rose flesh of dawn.
From her dew of lips, the drop of one word
Fell, from a dawn of fountains, when she murmured
"Darling"—upon my heart the song of the first bird.
"My dream glides in my dream," she said, "come true.
I waken from you to my dream of you."
O, then my waking dream dared to assume
The audacity of her sleep. Our dreams
Flowed into each other's arms, like streams.

TO NATASHA

You, whom such fragments do surround
    Of childhood straying through your face
Leaving two signs of hair there as your name—
    Through the loneliness
    Of my long look past the darkness
At the tunnel's end, I watch your curving neck,
The wondering colours marvel in your eyes,
My space of silence touch your dawn that lights
    My life's emerging line.

You, who are afraid of fear,
    Whose past has moulded hollows in your cheeks,
Who murmur "mercy", turning in your sleep,
    Whose glances touch me with shy voices:
        Your fingers of music
        Pressing down a rebellion of mistakes
Raise here our devout tower of mutual prayer.

I am one who knows each day his past
Tear out the links from an achieving chain;
    Daily through vigorous imagining
I summon my being again
    Out of a chaos of nothing.
My grasp on nothing builds my everything
Lest what I am should relapse into pieces.

Darling, this kiss of great serenity
Has cast no sheet anchor of security
    But balances upon the faith that lies
        In the timeless loving of your eyes
    Our terrible peace, where all that was

Certain and stated, falls apart
   Into original meanings, and the words
That weighed like boulders on us from the past
Are displaced by an earthquake of the heart.